No Matter What

There's Always Hope

TOMMYE WILLIAMS

WESTBOW
PRESS®
A DIVISION OF THOMAS NELSON
& ZONDERVAN

WestBow Press books may be ordered through booksellers or by contacting:

WestBow Press
A Division of Thomas Nelson & Zondervan
1663 Liberty Drive
Bloomington, IN 47403
www.westbowpress.com
844-714-3454

Scripture quotations marked NKJV are taken from the New King James Version.
Copyright © 1982 by Thomas Nelson, Inc. Used by permission. All rights reserved.

Scripture quotations marked NLT are taken from the Holy Bible,
New Living Translation, copyright © 1996, 2004, 2007 by Tyndale
House Foundation. Used by permission of Tyndale House Publishers,
Inc., Carol Stream, Illinois 60188. All rights reserved.

ISBN: 978-1-6642-9260-4 (sc)
ISBN: 978-1-6642-9261-1 (e)

Library of Congress Control Number: 2023903447

Print information available on the last page.

WestBow Press rev. date: 03/10/2023

CONTENTS

In memory of my beloved grandmother,
Mrs. Tommye J. Moore

PREFACE

My dear child, I want you to know that I am with you. I will never leave you nor forsake you. I am for you. I knew you even before I formed you in your mother's womb. I took delight in putting all the right pieces together when I formed you: your amazing and unique individuality, your smile, your personality, your gifts and talents … everything about you. You are My creation. You are My handiwork. You are Mine.

Your Heavenly Father

If you are reading this devotional, it is because the Lord wants you to have hope. Oftentimes extremely difficult childhood experiences leave us feeling hopeless or discouraged, and we feel stuck and can't imagine a future. But God wants you to look up and know that you are His child and you belong to Him. He wants you to know that you are loved and that you are not alone. He wants you to know that although others may have rejected you, He hasn't rejected you, and He never will reject you. He wants you to know that no matter what it looks like, no matter what you've been through, you can make it.

The fact that you were born is no accident. You are God's creation, and He created you on purpose. Your life has purpose. It's been said that life's disappointments can become divine appointments that lead us to God. So keep looking up. God's got a plan for your life.

Many a time they afflicted me from my youth,
Yet they have not prevailed against me. (Psalm 129:2)

The Bible says that children are a heritage from the Lord (Psalm 127:3). In other words, you are a divine blessing from God. You are special. You are significant. You matter. You have a future.

I know that at times you may feel pain, anger, hurt, or disappointment, or feel overlooked. You may feel that life has dealt you a bad hand. But God wants you to know that He sees you, He feels your pain, and He is with you. He wants you to know that He loves you with an everlasting love and you have a future and a hope.

> For I know the plans I have for you declares the Lord, plans to prosper you and not to harm you, to give you a future and a hope. (Jeremiah 29:11 NIV)

I have dedicated this devotional to my beloved grandmother, the late Mrs. Tommye J. Moore. She was a wonderful blessing in my life. She loved God with her whole heart all her life. She often told me a story about how, when she was just six years old, she told God, "God, if you're real, show me." And that night as she slept, God showed her the Garden of Eden in a dream. That next morning, she woke up the entire household and told them, "I told you, God is real." And she followed God wholeheartedly from that day forward.

Although there were many days as a schoolchild when my grandmother stayed in the restroom during lunchtime because she didn't have any lunch to eat, and although she grew up without a father, she was rich in faith, and God was the anchor of her life. She prospered in life and was a tremendous blessing not only to her family but to countless others. And throughout her life, my grandmother always had hope, no matter what came her way.

1

My Story

I should start by letting you know a little bit about me. There are a few painful parts to my story, from feeling disconnected and rejected as a child when my family moved to a new neighborhood and a girl spat in my face, to always being the last one to be chosen because I was a different race, to being afraid to be myself because I thought that no one would like the real me. I've always seen and felt the pain of others and carried the pain of others in my heart daily. I hid the real me and became invisible and blended in with everyone else. Although later on I developed friendships and was popular at school, I don't think anyone—except God—knew the real me. I thought the real me was not likable. I had rejected myself.

I had other challenges in my life after high school. I devoted my young adult years to a revolutionary organization that was a target of the FBI, and I got shot. I still have the scars and dents in my thighs from those days. I raised my son as a single parent and faced many unique challenges that single moms often face when raising sons, particularly during their son's teenage years, in the inner city. So I have had my share of life's ups and downs, but that's a topic for another time. Along with the tears I cried, I had many testimonies of God's goodness, and I always had an expectation that brighter days were ahead. I think that's why as a child I always loved the season of spring, because to me it symbolized a fresh start and a new beginning. It symbolized hope.

My story, God's plan for my life, continues to unfold, and I am excited about God's plans for me in this season. And I am excited about God's plans for you too. Your life story is still unfolding, so don't give up and don't despair. Brighter days are ahead, no matter what it may feel like right now.

My Assignment

I am on an assignment given to me by God. He wants me to tell you the good news that there is hope and that you shall win.

God chose me and assigned me to be the biological mother and a cheerleader for my son, Pastor Touré Thomas Roberts, who I mentioned earlier. Although he faced many challenges, including getting shot at the age of 16, God had a plan for his life. He is now a husband, father, pastor, author, and influential leader. I believe that God has also assigned me to be a mother figure or a cheerleader in other people's lives as well. And I believe that my assignment includes you. That's why you're reading this devotional. My assignment is to encourage you, to inspire hope in you, and most of all to point you to Jesus, who is your biggest fan and your biggest cheerleader. God assigned me to come after you and to let you know that no matter what you've been through or come out of, and no matter what you are currently facing—loneliness, abuse, rejection, low self-worth, or any other adversity—God is for you, He is with you, He is bigger than any circumstance you may face and you shall overcome all of these things.

I would be so very honored if you would allow me to be a mother figure or a cheerleader to you through the pages of this devotional. And just as I continually pray for my son, please know that I have already prayed for you. I prayed that you would be inspired to look up, look ahead, and look forward to your future with hope. I prayed that God's Truth would settle deep in your heart and that you would know the depths of His love for you. I prayed that you would know that God has not forsaken you, and I prayed that His Word would become the anchor of your life. And I am praying that you will see yourself as God sees you. That you will know that you have great value and great worth. That you will have hope for your future.

2

WHAT IS HOPE?

Before I give you some definitions of hope, I'd love for you to think about and to write or draw what the word "hope" means to you. So please take a moment to use the space below to write down your thoughts or to draw to show what hope means to you.

What Hope Means to Me

Here are a few additional meanings or definitions for hope for you to consider:

- belief, faith, or confidence in the expectation of something
- the capacity to trust in, wait for, look for, or expect something good in the future
- the belief that the future can be better than the past

- looking forward not based on what you've gone through but based on the Word of God
- the ability to look at any situation and know that regardless of how it may appear, God is going to come through

For me, hope is trusting in the goodness and faithfulness of God no matter what. In my old church, we used to sing a hymn that said,

> My hope is built on nothing less
> than Jesus Christ and His righteousness.
> On Christ the solid rock I stand,
> all other ground is sinking sand.

Hope is knowing that we can look at any situation through eyes focused on what God's Word says. Hope is having confidence that God will come through. That is the truth I live by. That is my testimony.

Hope: God's Battle Plan for Victory

You and I have an enemy. Some may call him the devil, some may call him Satan, and others may call him that dirty ol' rascal. But regardless of what we call him, he is the Enemy. He is a thief. He starts trying to rob us of hope in our early childhood through the adverse experiences we face that cause wounds—sometimes physical, sometimes mental, sometimes emotional, and sometimes all of the above. These wounds are caused by difficulties and hardships we experience. And as we get older, we often carry those past wounds with us.

Wounds from our past can cause hurt, anger, disappointment, sadness, pain, and lack of hope or hopelessness. But God wants us to hold onto hope no matter what our circumstances look like. He wants you to know that He sees you, He knows you, and He will come through. Luke 12:7 says:

The very hairs of your head are all numbered. Don't
be afraid. You are worth more than many sparrows.

Now that's some good news! And here's some more good news.
(Drum roll, please …)

The Fight Is Fixed

Jesus tells us, "In this world we will have tribulation, but be of good
cheer, for I have overcome the world" (John 16:33). In other words,
although we are in a battle, the fight is already fixed. The winner has
already been declared. Jesus conquered death, hell, and the grave on
our behalf, and He rose from the dead with all power in His hands.
And through Jesus we, too, have the victory. The fight is fixed in
our favor! We win!

But that doesn't mean that we won't face difficulties and
challenges, affliction and adverse circumstances. What it does
mean is that we can overcome these things. We are more than
conquerors through Jesus Christ. God's Word says, "But thanks be
to God which gives us the victory through Jesus Christ our Lord"
(1 Corinthians 15:57).

And although the fight is fixed and we ultimately win, we still
must fight.

How We Win

Here's how we win.

We win by being patient and holding onto hope, no matter what
it looks like.

We win by loving ourselves.

We win by casting down the negative thoughts and toxic beliefs
we have about ourselves in our minds, by replacing those thoughts

with God's Truth about who we are, and by believing that we are worthy of being loved and that our lives have value.

We win by believing in and standing on God's Word.

We win by choosing the future over the past.

We win by acknowledging and being truthful about how we feel. If we feel pain, hurt, anger, sadness, grief, or we feel an ache in our heart, we can pour out our heart to God and tell God all about how we're feeling instead of keeping it locked up inside. This is called *lamentation*. But we don't stay stuck there. We lament and then we look up.

We win by having confidence that brighter days are ahead for us.

We win by setting goals for our lives because we know we have a future.

We win by coming up with a plan to achieve the goals we establish because we know our life has value.

We win by celebrating our wins, whether they are big wins or small wins.

We win by not being ashamed to hope because we know that our life matters. As music artist and actor Trevor Jackson says in one of his songs, "there's a place for your face in this world." The world is waiting on you.

We win by silencing that negative inner critic that says "I can't" and replace that voice with "I can do all things through Christ."

Most of all, we win by trusting in God, who is our Heavenly Father, and by knowing that God's Son Jesus is on our side.

Jesus is our Savior, Jesus is our Advocate. Jesus is our Champion. Jesus is our biggest cheerleader.

Come to Jesus

Young people are precious to Jesus, and that includes you. When Jesus spoke before the huge crowds, He told His disciples, "Let the children come to me. Do not hinder them" (Matthew 19:14). Jesus wants you to come to Him. He wants you to invite Him into your heart to be your Lord and Savior. He wants you to get to know Him and to know how much He loves you. Jesus wants you to keep your head up and to have hope.

Because of great love, Jesus left His home in heaven and came to earth to save us. That's why He's called the Savior. The depth and magnitude of His love was demonstrated when He died on the Cross for us.

> Greater love hath no man than this, that a man lay down His life for His friends. (John 15:13)

3

HOPE CARRIERS FROM THE BIBLE

In this chapter and the next, you will meet four people who lived during biblical times and four people from current times, all of whom experienced pain, hurt, or disappointment in their early years but trusted in God and held on to hope—and God came through. Some from our own time are still holding on to hope as their life story continues to unfold, and God is with them each step of the way.

Four Biblical Hope Carriers

Let's start by meeting four people from the Bible.

Jabez: Pain Is Not My Name

You can meet Jabez in 1 Chronicles 4:10.

Jabez was born in obscurity. He wasn't born into fame or power. No one knew who Jabez was when he was born. In other words, he was not noticed.

When his mother gave birth to him, she named him Jabez, which means "he makes sorrow." Can you imagine someone being named Sorrow? That could be very hard to deal with. That name might make some people feel ashamed. But the Bible says that Jabez prayed and asked God to bless him and enlarge his territory, and it was God's good pleasure to bless Jabez. Jabez believed in God, and God granted him what he asked.

Sometimes you may feel unnoticed and discouraged, but God wants you to be like Jabez and trust Him. Do not be afraid to ask Him to help you and to do great things through you.

Remember: *pain is not your name.*
Have you ever felt that you have greatness inside of you but feel discouraged because noone seems to notice your greatness? You don't have to answer this question right away. Think about it and come back later and write or draw about what great things you would like to do with God's help.

Joseph: Fruitful in the Land of My Affliction

You can meet Joseph in Genesis, chapters 37 through 50.

Joseph was one of Jacob's twelve sons. Joseph's father gave him a coat of many colors. His brothers were jealous of him. They threw him into a pit and left him to die. He got out of the pit but was sold into slavery. Later he was falsely accused of raping his master's wife and sent to prison.

But even in the pit and in prison, Joseph always had faith in God. He had hope as his anchor, and he waited on God. Even in the most difficult circumstances, he did what was right and pleasing in God's sight, and God was with him. God made Joseph fruitful in the land where he had endured adversity and affliction.

Joseph had favor with Pharaoh, the ruler of Egypt, and Pharaoh appointed him second in command because of Joseph's wisdom and righteous behavior. Many years after Joseph's brothers threw him into the pit, he was in a position to help them, and he was glad to do so. He told them, "What you meant for evil, God turned it around for good to save many people."

Like Joseph, you may find yourself in unfair circumstances, but ultimately, what was meant for evil, God will turn around for good. With God, you will not only survive but thrive in the midst of your difficult circumstances. And your life will be a blessing to countless others.

Remember: *you too can do great things even in the land of your affliction.*

Write or create a drawing about what it feels like to be in a pit and something you could do after God helps you out of the pit.

David: The Lord Is My Keeper

You can meet David mainly in First and Second Samuel, First and Second Chronicles, and in several of the Psalms.

David was a shepherd boy who became Israel's most important king. He was the youngest of eight sons. Being the youngest, he was often overlooked. When he was a boy, his job was to tend the sheep. Most likely, he was a loner, and most times he was isolated from the others.

When David became a teenager, he was anointed by God through the prophet Samuel to be Israel's next king. When God gave the prophet Samuel the assignment to anoint Israel's next king, at first the prophet Samuel overlooked David and first went to each of David's brothers. But God let Samuel know that the brothers were not the one that He had chosen. David was. God told Samuel, "Man looks at the outer appearance, I look at the heart."

David loved God with all his heart. He wrote many songs of praise to God, and he also wrote many cries for help. What I especially love about David is that he always poured out his heart to God when he was in trouble or feeling overwhelmed. And he always had hope in God.

Although it seemed like David had been overlooked, God chose him to be anointed as Israel's next king. And while many years passed before David became king, those early years were a season of preparation. During those years, David learned that "if God is for me, who can be against me?" And that's a promise for you as well.

You may feel like it's been a long time that you have been waiting for the hardships to end, but God is for you. He has a plan for your life, and His plan shall come to pass.

In one of the Psalms that people all over the world know and love (Psalm 23), verse 1 begins with the words "The Lord is My Shepherd" (Psalm 23). And a shepherd keeps watch over his sheep. The Lord had been David's keeper—in other words, He watched over David—all the days of his life.

Remember: *God is your keeper.*
Consider and write or draw about how God acting on your behalf might prevent you from feeling isolated.

Hagar: God Sees Me

You can meet Hagar in Genesis, chapters 16 and 21.

Hagar was an Egyptian slave girl. She was Sarah's maidservant. Hagar experienced much pain and hardship as a servant, but she was seen by God in all her hurt and all the bitterness of her soul. Her pain and bitterness was caused by Sarah and Abraham taking matters into their own hands instead of waiting on God to give them their promised son. Sarah convinced Abraham to have a child by Hagar, but after several years, Sarah ultimately became jealous and told Abraham to send Hagar and her son away.

So Hagar and her son were sent away with only small rations of food and water, not enough to keep them alive for long. But God sent an angel to them, and they were miraculously saved from dying of hunger and thirst.

During the two most painful times in Hagar's life, God spoke out loud to her. How amazing is that! And both times God spoke to Hagar, He addressed her pain and provided hope for her. When God spoke to Hagar after Abraham sent her and her son away, He let her know that He saw her, that He had not forgotten her, and that He had a plan for her and her son. He told her that her son would never be enslaved as she had been and that she would have many descendants through her son.

God wants you to know that He sees you, just as he saw Hagar; He has not forgotten you, and He has plans for your future.

Hagar is the first human being to give God a new name. She called Him *El Roi*, which means "the God who sees me."

Remember: *God sees you.*

Sometimes things happen in life that are unfair. Have you ever felt that way? How does it feel to know that God sees you and has a plan for you? Write your answer here.

4

TODAY'S HOPE CARRIERS

Now let's meet our four hope carriers from today. I asked them to share their stories so you can hear them in their own words.

They all faced adversity in their early years, and some are facing adversity even today, but they are hope carriers—and God has been and continues to be with them each step of their journey. Just as God has plans for their future, He has plans for you.

Kyrsten: It's Dope to Hope

Meet Kyrsten, age nineteen.

My family history is rooted in hurt and abandonment, yet I can see the generational curse being broken with every generation. My understanding of my great-grandmother's story is that she was not raised by her mother—my great-great grandmother—for the first fifteen years of her life. But when my great-grandmother was fifteen, her mother married, and my great-grandmother went to live with her mother. But the husband never accepted or tried to include my great-grandmother in any family-related matters, and her mother either never knew or turned a blind eye to the situation.

I believe this is the reason why my great-grandmother never got married. I also believe that her poor relationship with her mother transitioned into the relationships with her daughters because she didn't know how to be a mother. But through her brokenness, I believe that her refusal to get married was a subconscious way of protecting her two daughters. My grandma is one of her daughters, and may or may not have broken a generational curse.

My grandma, though she was not only mentally ill but also a single mother, made sure that she was the one raising her five children. Though she was extremely abusive both verbally and mentally, she made sure that she was always there for her children, unlike her mother (my great-grandmother), who let her children be raised by their grandmother. Another generational chain was broken.

In addition, my grandma unintentionally created an atmosphere so that her children had the support she never had, which is reflected in the strong bond between her children. And in God's favor, He had presented her children with additional support, which was in the blessing of kindness and empathy of others.

As for my mother, even though like the generations before her, she did not select the best partner at the age of eighteen, when I was born, yet she not only made sure that she raised me in a safe environment but also was not verbally or mentally abusive, in addition to giving her children a good father figure later on. A generational curse is broken.

So for myself, I hope and know that I will not only choose the partner the first time but will raise my children in an amazing environment.

Now that I have written the previous passage, I realize that as each generation's relationship with God grew, the more the generational chains were broken. For a further explanation from the recollection, my great-grandmother is not religious, assuming that when was a child she went to church like many others but she never truly sought after God. In recent years she does not go to church, nor do I believe that she prays unless she is going through hardships. My grandma is a constant church attendee, and I do believe that she truly seeks God. But when I say that she seeks God, I mean that she only seeks enough to solve her surface needs and problems yet does not seek to heal her soul. Maybe she doesn't know how to ask for true healing, or maybe she is so comfortable in her pain that she no longer seeks healing. She no longer seeks healing, just like her mother, but I do believe that she is closer to God.

As I look upon my grandma's life, I see that though she was far from a "suitable" parent, God had great favor upon her life, as she raised five children: two sons, both veterans; two daughters who gave her six grandkids; and one daughter who takes care of her. Though they have their own wounds in different ways, they all turned out to be amazing children.

My mother was exposed to the church by her mother and another guardian. I believe that my mother's guardian's guidance really gave her the foundation of the Lord, and though she had her bumps in the road, she turned out well. I believe she was able to break free of the generational chains because she was not only raised in a house of God but also learned how to serve the Lord.

As for me, I was born in the Lord. All I know is the Lord, which I believe is the reason why I have grace and favor upon my life. Though my mother has broken generational chains, I am happy that I have broken a few myself and strive to continue setting my family free as I find my purpose.

Remember: *to have hope is dope!*

Treasdreonia: Not Forsaken

Meet Treasdreonia, age thirty.

Tasha Cobbs Leonard's song "The Church I Grew Up In" speaks volumes of testament in my life! The lyric says:

There is healing in these walls
There's angels dancing down these halls
If it's Wednesday night or Sunday morning
We don't need much, 'cause Jesus loves it
If you wanna know where my history began
If you wanna know why I am the way I am
It's the church I grew up in

Growing up in the church has really shaped the way I live my life. Thirty years have not seemed that long on this earth, but it has been worth the roller-coaster ride. I grew up in a Christian home and went to church nearly every day, including Sundays. My membership at Greater Ebenezer Missionary Baptist Church, located in Los Angeles, California; has been the building foundation of who I am today.

I was a faithful member of many ministries, I participated in many church events, but most importantly I was given the basic instructions and tools to live a life pleasing to God. Most may say that nothing about church really clicked for them at a young age, or it almost felt like it was a forced practice that they had to do because their parents made them do it. But being a member of GEMBC, I never felt that way. Those really were the best days of my life!

Growing up in the church was my foundation, my home, my safe haven, my support, and my family. The church walls were filled with the prayers of my praying grandmother, my mother, all the church mothers and fathers, my pastor, and the teachers. Those prayers and cries to God for the youth were the protection that helped guide us to be of the world and not in the world.

As I look back on all those great years, great memories flood my mind. The most important memories are about those individuals who made a huge impact in my life and how those impacts have shaped my life forever.

Life for me hasn't always been easy. I have had to face many adversities and learn a lot about life by taking risks and falling in the process. I didn't come from a two-parent home, nor did we have a lot of money. I envied others who had that, and I desired a life like theirs. During the most vital stage in my life, I had to endure a lot of loss. At that young age, I thought I was the reason why those individuals were gone.

No matter what life has brought my way, I am grateful for my past because it has led me to find my strength. I had a village of amazing individuals who loved me and supported me. In places where I felt most lonely or when life seemed dark, no matter what, the devil never won, because I had a praying army covering me. Those tough times have definitely made me a stronger woman, and they have turned into my greatest life lessons. In the midst of those most difficult moments, I have always continued to press forward.

Even after I left for college, my relationship with God grew immensely. My late pastor emeritus Dr. Solomon L. Drake used to say that "there are two things no one can take from you. That's the love of Jesus Christ and a good education." Throughout my entire college career, I instilled that message into my life.

When I was in college, there was a year when the school told me that I did not have enough money to continue my education. I said "but God." That summer I had to move off campus because tuition was too high. No matter what, God still provided. Because of my faith the size of a mustard seed, I received free housing for being a part of the school's summer program, and I worked two jobs. I was determined to find help to keep me in school, so I stayed, visiting the financial aid office every single day. I wanted to graduate from college so bad that I could taste it on the tip of my tongue. I would persistently go to the financial aid office until I spoke to someone who had the most power to help me. Each day I prayed, and I was tested by life, but I would always choose God over worldly temptations that tried to distract me.

At the beginning of the summer, I owed the school $26,000 to stay in school. When I moved off campus, I owed $15,000. Finally, I was able to speak with someone in financial aid, and they knocked my balance down to $10,000. At the end of the program, I knew I still needed more money but did not know where it was going to come from. Our program leader instructed us to go to the gym to handle any financial aid issues before we had our last meeting.

So I went to the gym, and for some reason my feet took me to the validation line. The validation line is for students who have paid for their tuition in full. My mind kept asking me why I was in that line, but my soul told me that I needed to stay in that line.

I got to the front of the line, and the lady asked me to swipe my ID card. She then proceeded to say, "Your balance is $120."

Mind you, I owed another $10,000! I said, "Is that all I owe? Because I can pay that right now."

She said, "No, sweetheart, that's how much the school owes you!"

I dropped to my knees and started crying and worshiping God.

No matter what you are faced with and no matter how bad it seems, if you put your faith in God, God will bless you beyond your heart's desires. I stand here today having graduated with my bachelor's of science from Virginia State University.

Now that I am much older, I am much wiser, and my faith in God is stronger. As I walk into the next chapter of my life, I can't wait to see what God has in store for me. As I look back over my life, I can honestly say that I am proud of the woman I have become. I thank God, who is the head of my life. I thank Him for His love, His protection, His mercy, and His grace! Without God by my side, where would I be?

I am truly blessed to also have the love and support from many loved ones, along with the teachings and foundation I received from church—I am who I am because of that!

Sister Williams, if I could express to you all the reasons that I am grateful for you, it could take me days to say. I admire your servant's heart because it is God's work of art. Your dedication, hard work, love, care, support, and compassion have been a blessing to many lives you have touched. Giving the best of yourself in the good and bad times is a true testament to the beauty of your soul. My heart is full of my perpetual appreciation for you and the acts of service you aspire to do each day. Words cannot describe how proud I am of you for pursuing the dream that God has put on your heart. You have taken a leap of faith and moved in the steps of obedience, but most importantly, you believe in God for equipping you for the work and seeing you through. You are a phenomenal and amazing woman of God!

I am honored to have known you since I was a little girl, and I am so blessed to still have you as an important part of my life. Your love and support have shaped me in so many ways. Thank you for everything you are and what you have been to me. May God continue to pour into you as His vessel, and may He continue to bless you and your family! I love you with my whole heart.

Remember: *you are not forsaken.*

Gabby: Beauty from Ashes

Meet Gabby, age thirty-eight.

I was born into a family with an abusive mother who struggled with mental illness and an absentee father. Living in the projects of South Los Angeles was in no way encouraging. The environment we lived in was low-income and poverty-stricken, and although most of the people living there were poor, my family was one of the poorest in the community. Life was hard. My mother struggled to care for her five children, and we had social worker after social worker constantly involved in our lives from the continual reports of abuse and neglect the Department of Children and Family Services received. We often ran out of food and had to go to the food banks or reach out to family members for help.

In many ways, I didn't get the opportunity to just be a kid and experience that childlike wonder that I grew up watching on the television. My mother did the best she could, but as her children we had to learn how to fend for ourselves and one another. It was imperative to my survival to hold on to the hope that this would not last always. And I held on.

Without faith and relying on scriptures of hope in those times of lack, in those times of hardship, in those times of fear, I am not sure where I would be today. Hope kept me and sustained me. I knew that if I held on long enough, relief would eventually come. Hope allowed me to view all the things that I, at the time, hated about my life through the lens of compassion and gratitude. I learned to appreciate my circumstances for they has contributed to the woman I am today—and I would not change that for the world.

Remember: *God can make beauty from the ashes of your life.*

Corion: We Walk by Faith

Meet Corion, age fifteen.

I was born in the summer of 2007. I was born and raised in Long Beach, California. I lost hope when my mom and dad broke up. It was very challenging seeing other kids living in a two-parent home, and I grew up in a single-parent home.

Some days we would not have food, and my mom would cry just thinking of ways to feed me and my brother. It was hard seeing my momma cry, and then I realized my dad was a gang member, and I started to get curious about the things I saw growing up as a kid. My mom started taking me to church, and then I started hanging out with my cousins. Their dad is a gang member, so I was exposed to it. My mom did not know what I was doing at first, and then she seen I started to change.

Hanging out with my cousins, my behavior changed. I started to talk back, and I started getting into fights. Then I realized that was not the life I wanted, and when you get too deep, there's no turning back. I used to heard my mom cry and pray to God, hoping I would take a different route. Once time, the next day I went over there and told them I didn't wanna hang out and be affiliated with that. I came home I prayed with my mom. She started taking me to church faithfully, and my life turned around. I started going to the gym, working out and boxing with my uncle. I'm now a football player.

When you turn your life around, best believe there will be challenges, and you will have to face them and just have faith. That's what I did, because my mom taught me that with faith anything is possible. Everything in my life is going in the right direction. My parents may not be together, but I get to see my dad on the weekends, and everything in life is going great.

When you listen to your parents, you will be able to do stuff you thought you would never be able to do. Your parents would never tell you anything wrong or wanna see you fail. Like my mom didn't wanna see me fail—she had faith in me and never gave up on me, and for that I'm thankful and grateful. I know God has amazing plans for me, and He also has amazing plans for you who are reading this as well.

Remember: *walk by faith and not by sight, no matter what it may look or feel like.*

Can I Become a Hope Carrier?

Now that you've met eight outstanding hope carriers, you may be wondering whether you too could become a hope carrier. And the answer is yes!

The biggest part of being a hope carrier is to know that you are loved by God, that He created you on purpose, that you are valuable, and that God's plan for you is to give you a future and a hope. Next steps are for you to write down some things about how God made you, and then to think about and write down some steps or goals you'd like to establish for your immediate future. You'll find some directions at the end of this book to get you started. But first, let's learn more about having the truth of God's Word in your life.

5

GOD'S WORD IS TRUTH

I live my life with a firm belief in the truth of God's Word. That is the foundation I build my life on. Most of all, Jesus knew how important it is for us to know that God's Word is true.

In John 17, we find Jesus praying to His Father for His friends, the disciples, because He knew He would be leaving them and going back to heaven soon. He prayed about the things that were most important for the disciples to live by—for the disciples to know that God's Word is truth and that they should continue to love God, to love one another and to be one.

Jesus knew that God's Word would be as important today as it was thousands of years ago. God's Word stands forever. His Word is Truth. And when we have faith in God and stand on His Word, He will always come through. This is the truth that I live by.

> Let us hold fast to our profession of faith without wavering, for He is faithful that promised. (Hebrews 10:23)

So when the Enemy attacks your mind and your thoughts, push back against his lie, and replace the lie and the negative thought with the Word of God. God's Word is truth.

Your Devotions

Devotions, also called devotional thoughts, are a way to connect you to the heart of God. The more you connect to God, the more you receive His peace, His joy and hope for any challenge you may be facing. Devotions usually include a Bible verse on a specific topic followed by a thought or message on that topic to lift your spirits when you feel discouraged or hopeless. The devotions I prepared for you have a quotation from the Bible to reflect on, a related message, and a prayer. Following are eight devotional thoughts as well as some decrees and affirmations you can tell yourself daily. There are devotions for each day of the week and a bonus devotion (Devotion 8). I think it would be great if you read the Bonus Devotion every day along with the devotion for each day of the week.

Take your time to read and reflect on these devotional thoughts when you feel down or hopeless. It is part of the battle plan. The prayer at the end of each devotion is based on God's Word. I included these scripture-based prayers because that's the strategy I use when I pray for my son. I pray God's Word straight from the Bible, and God is faithful to keep His Word. So as you read these devotions, I pray that you will allow God's Truths to take root and settle deep in your heart, thoughts, and mind.

Day 1. My Safe Place

My God is my Rock, in whom I take refuge, my shield and the horn of my salvation.
He is my stronghold, my refuge and my savior from violent people You save me. (2 Samuel 22:3 NIV)

Remember David, whom you met earlier? These words were written by him. David loved God and always poured out his heart to God. God was his keeper. God was his safe place.

God wants to be your safe place too. When an enemy tries to come against you by attacking your mind with negative thoughts and lies or by inflicting painful and difficult circumstances, you can run to God for safety. He is your safe place. And whenever you run to Him, He is ready to protect you.

You might wonder how we run to God. What does running to God look like? Running to God actually means to stop and to go to God in prayer about all your concerns, fears, and anxiety, then trust that God will see you through.

God will always be a safe place for you to run to. You can trust Him with your deepest thoughts and concerns.

"Safe Place" Prayer
Psalm 56:3

God, thank You for being my safe place. Thank You for being my protector. When I feel overwhelmed or afraid, I will put my trust in you. In Jesus's name, amen.

Day 2. My Help

> Do not fear for I am with you. Don't be dismayed for I am your God. I will help you. I will strengthen you. I will hold you up with my powerful right hand. (Isaiah 41:10)

God wants you to know that He will help you and strengthen you when you go through hard times. He tells us that we don't need to be afraid, that He will hold us in His hands. So hold on to God's unchanging and capable Hand. He is your ever-present help.

"My Help" Prayer
Proverbs 18:10

Lord, I don't have to be afraid, because you are holding me, you are helping me, and you are keeping me safe even in the middle of a storm. You are my strong tower. I run to You and am safe. In Jesus's name, amen.

Day 3. My Hope

And now Lord, what do I wait for?
My hope is in You. (Psalm 39:7)

So many times in the Bible, God tells us to have hope: hope in Him, hope in His Word, and hope in His Son Jesus. Hope is about believing in the best for your future. We know that God's plans for your future are good, no matter what it may look like right now. So always have hope.

"My Hope" Prayer
Psalm 71:14

Lord, although things sometimes feel a little shaky, I choose to put my hope in You. I am thankful that You are with me and that Your Word is true. I know You love me and that You will keep Your promise. Thank You for Your faithfulness. In Jesus's name, amen.

Day 4. My Purpose

For we know that in all things God works for the good of those who love Him, for those who have been called according to His Purpose. (Romans 8:28)

What do you dream of doing as you get older? Do you think of a career you want to have or a passion you want to pursue? God has a purpose for your life. That's why He created you. There's a place for your face in the earth.

You might not know what your purpose in life is right now, but you will find it. Think about things you love to do, and love God with all your heart. You will eventually find your purpose.

"My Purpose" Prayer
Isaiah 43:7

Thank You, Lord, for creating me on purpose. I am not an accident. I am not a mistake. You created me on purpose. There is a job that You want me to do. Thank You for the gifts and talents you have placed in me. Help me to use them for Your glory. In Jesus's name, amen.

Day 5. My Promise

> When you pass through the waters, I will be with you; and when you pass through the rivers, they will not sweep over you. When you walk through the fire, you will not be burned; the flames will not set you ablaze. For I am the Lord, Your God. The Holy One of Israel, your Savior. (Isaiah 43:2–3 NIV)

Sometimes you feel like you're in deep waters or in the midst of a fire and that you are all alone. But God is with you, He loves you, and you will make it through. Nothing can separate you from God's love. Absolutely nothing. So do not despair. God is on your side. And that's a promise!

"My Promise" Prayer
Romans 8:38, Jeremiah 31:3, Deuteronomy 31:6

Dear Lord, I am thankful that You love me with an everlasting love and that nothing shall ever separate me from your love. You will never leave me nor forsake me. In Jesus's name, amen.

Day 6. My Comfort

> Blessed be God, even the Father of our Lord Jesus Christ, the Father of mercies, and the God of all comfort. (2 Corinthians 1:3)

Comfort is what we need when sad or painful things happen or when we have feelings of grief. We need to be able to pour out our feelings to someone. Sometimes we don't have anyone nearby right at the moment when we most need comfort. But remember that God is always there. He neither slumbers nor sleeps. You can pour out your heart to Him at any time, night or day. He will hear you and comfort you with His presence.

"My Comfort" Prayer
Psalm 147:3

Dear Lord, I am thankful that I can draw near to you and You will draw near to me. I am thankful that I can pour out my heart to you and that you will heal my broken heart and bind up my wounds. In Jesus's name, amen.

Day 7. My Support

> When I said "my foot is slipping" your unfailing love, Lord, supported me. When anxiety was great within me, Your consolation brought me joy. (Psalm 94:18–19 NIV)

You know what snow is like: you can slip on it pretty easily. You can be walking one minute and then falling on the ground the next minute.

Life can sometimes give us hard things that make us feel like we are on slippery snow. Without God's help, we will fall over. The Enemy wants us to slip into anger, fear, and doubt. At those times when you feel that you're falling or slipping, call out to God. Hold to His unchanging Hand. He will keep you from falling.

Prayer
Isaiah 59:1

Dear Lord, I am thankful that Your Hand is not so short that it cannot save me and that You will not let my foot slip. In Jesus's name, amen.

8. My Future (A Bonus Devotional Thought)

> There is surely a future hope for you and your hope
> will not be cut off.
> (Proverbs 23:18 NIV)

God made you. Carefully and beautifully, He made you. And He knew exactly what He was doing and why.

The next time you wonder whether you are good enough, remember that you are God's handiwork and that you're more than enough because God made you. And if you ever feel shame or guilt about things that happened in your past, please know that those feelings are not from God. So turn those feelings over to God and replace them with God's Truth. You are loved. You are valued. You are cherished, and you are worthy of love.

God's love for you never changes when you do or experience things that seem to fall short of God's plan. The Bible tells us that

God sent His Son Jesus not to condemn the world but that the world through Jesus might be saved (John 3:17). There is nothing that can separate you from God's love.

"My Future" Prayer
Jeremiah 29:11

Dear Lord, I am thankful that You created me on purpose and that the plans you have for me are good. Thank You that I have a future and a hope. In Jesus's Name. Amen.

DECREES AND AFFIRMATIONS

God's Word is your truth. I know I keep repeating these words, and that's because I want that truth to settle deep down into your heart, into your mind, and into your thoughts. So many times I have stood on God's Word during extremely difficult and challenging times, and God has always come through for me. He will do the same for you when you stand on His Word.

I know that the Enemy always tries to sneak into your thoughts and mind, and sometimes your own inner voice tells you that you can't. But I want you to fight back. The following affirmations and decrees will help you.

These decrees and affirmations are all based on God's Word. Sometimes the answers may take longer than you'd like, but God will keep His Word. That's a promise.

Affirmations are statements you say out loud to yourself to be reminded of the things that are true about you. Decrees are statements you make more broadly to yourself, others, and the Enemy. That's how you establish your authority.

Make these statements out loud! Say them daily. Say them, and believe them! That's how you kick the Enemy to the curb and out of your thoughts. This is your truth to say daily.

Six Affirmations

1. I am amazing and wonderfully made. (Psalm 139:14)
2. I am loved with an everlasting love. (Jeremiah 31:3)
3. I am created for God's glory. (Isaiah 43:7)
4. I am created for a purpose. (Jeremiah 1:5)
5. I am God's masterpiece. (Ephesians 2:10)
6. I am more than a conqueror. (Romans 8:37)

Four Decrees

1. Even if my mother or father forsake me, I am not an orphan. (Psalm 27:10)
2. No weapon formed against me shall prosper. (Isaiah 54:17)
3. I can do all things through Christ who strengthens me. (Philippians 4:13)
4. I have the victory through Jesus Christ my Lord. (1 Corinthians 15:57)

6

BECOMING A HOPE CARRIER

I am excited about you and the plans God has for you. The best is yet to come! So keep looking up, hold on to hope, and have faith in God. You are an overcomer and will not be disappointed. I want you to know that I think you are amazing! I think you are wonderful! And I am so very proud of you for hanging in there and reading this devotional all the way to the end. That is a great accomplishment. You rock!

And as your life story continues onward and upward, I encourage you to do four things that God instructs us to do in His Word. The first three come from Romans 12:12, and the fourth from Hebrews 10:23.

1. Be joyful in hope.
2. Be patient during hard times.
3. Be faithful in prayer.
4. Hold fast to faith in God and His Word, because God is faithful to keep His promises.

HOPE SCRIPTURES

As you discover God's plan for you, and know the depths of God's love for you, you will become a hope carrier. These scriptures will help you hold on to hope.

I am the Lord, those who hope in Me, shall not be disappointed. (Isaiah 49:23)

Be of good courage,
and He shall strengthen your heart,
all that hope in Your Word. (Psalm 31:24)

You are my hiding place and my shield.
I hope in your Word. (Psalm 119:114)

There is hope for your future declares the Lord and your children shall come back to their own country. (Jeremiah 31:17)

Christ in me. The hope of glory. (Colossians 1:27)

The Lord shall also roar out of Zion, and utter His voice from Jerusalem, and the heavens and earth shall shake, but the Lord will be the hope of His people. (Joel 3:16)

Those who hope in the Lord shall renew their strength. (Isaiah 40:31)

For You are my hope Oh Lord,
my confidence from my youth. (Psalm 71:5)

Behold, the eye of the Lord is upon them that fear
[respect and reverence] Him, for those who hope in
His unfailing love. (Psalm 33:18)

It is good to both hope and wait for the salvation of
the Lord. (Lamentations 3:26)

Why are you cast down oh my soul,
and why so disturbed within?
Put your hope in God,
for I will yet praise Him,
my Savior and my God. (Psalm 42:5)

Guide me in Your Truth and teach me,
for You are my God, my Savior,
and my hope is in You all day long. (Psalm 25:5)

MY CLOSING THOUGHTS FOR YOU

As I close, I want you to know that I wrote this devotional just
for you. Yes, *you*. You were in my heart and on my mind when
I wrote it. So I would love for you to keep this devotional book
handy and to read it often. Always remember that I am cheering
for you, and I will continue cheering and praying for you. I believe
and decree that you will be a hope carrier and that you will have
praise reports and testimonies, just like the hope carriers you met
earlier in this devotional. And just like one of the current hope
carriers in this devotional, I believe that you can be the one to break
negative generational patterns in your family. I believe you can be
the solution. I believe in you.

Please be sure to write down a few of your immediate goals
on the pages provided at the end of this book and be sure to tell
someone about your goals. They'll be cheering you on too. And

I believe that you will come up with a plan of action to help you achieve your goals. I know you can do it, and I am cheering you on. But most of all, Jesus will be cheering for you. He is your biggest cheerleader and your biggest fan. In other words, you've got plenty of backup, and you SHALL win!

As our time together comes to a close, I want you to know that I will forever keep you in my heart. I hope that I have fulfilled my assignment as a mother figure and a cheerleader to you through the pages of this devotional; that you feel loved, supported, and encouraged; and that you have renewed hope for the days ahead. I pray that you will hold on to hope and that it will be the anchor for your soul.

I pray that if you haven't already done so, you will invite Jesus into your life as your Lord and Savior. He is waiting for you with His arms opened wide. And I pray that no matter what, you will always remember that you belong to God, that He will never reject you, that you are created by God, accepted by God, and deeply loved by God, that He is your Heavenly Father, and that your realization of His perfect love for you will cast out any fear or doubt you may have about your future. I pray that you will always remember that God is your safe place, and He will never leave you nor forsake you.

Because I know that praying God's Word brings results, and if we ask anything according to His will, He hears us (1st John 5:14) I close with this prayer for you.

Dear Heavenly Father,

I ask You, the God of hope, to fill each person reading this book with all joy and peace as they trust in You, so that they may overflow with hope by the power of the Holy Spirit. I pray that you will give them beauty for ashes, the oil of joy for mourning and a garment of praise for a spirit of heaviness. I pray that they will know the heights and depths of Your love for them and that they will know that nothing can separate them from Your love. I pray that they will know in their hearts that Your Word is Truth and that Your Word will be their sure foundation. I thank You Lord that they will know You as their Abba (Heavenly Father) and that they will know that all things are possible with You. I pray that they will always hold on to hope, no matter what. I thank You that You cause all things to work together for good for those who love You and are called according to Your purpose and that each and every person reading this book has a future and a hope.

In Jesus's name I pray. And it is so. Amen.

Starting Your Journey as a Hope Carrier

Now that you are ready to become a hope carrier, I'd like you to answer some questions that are all about you and how God created you. I'd like you to think about what you like to do, what you good at, what you are interested in, and what your desire is for future. Are there some goals you can see yourself achieving w the next month or two? What are your strengths? What a proud of about yourself?

So please take some time to think through the All A questions on the next page and to write down your answ you'll be ready for the goal setting activity.

_____: All About Me
your name

I am interested in

I am good at

My strengths are

I am proud of myself because

Something I would like to improve in is

2 or 3 immediate goals that I have for myself are

What I like about me is

Challenges or obstacles I face are

I can overcome these obstacles by

Fears I sometimes have are

My dream or vision (my aspiration) for my future is

Something super special or unique about me is

SETTING MY GOALS

Now it would be awesome if you wrote down a couple of your immediate goals. The following page will help you map them out. Please use one goal for each page. It would be super awesome if you would share your goals with someone and ask them to help you stay on track. So please tell someone about your goals! They'd love to cheer you on. And I am cheering for you too!

"The only person you are destined to become is the person you decide to be"

Ralph Waldo Emerson

W I S E GOALS

MY MAIN GOAL RIGHT NOW

MY NO.1 GOAL IS...

TARGET DATE

How will I know I've reached my goal?

My key strengths that will help me achieve this goal are...
1.
2.
3.
4.
5.

This goal is important to me because...

Obstacles that may arise are...
1.
2.
3.
4.
5.

How I plan to respond to each obstacle:

What will be different when I achieve my goal?

NEXT BEST STEPS
1.
2.
3.
4.
5.

© wisegoals.com

"The only person you are destined to become is the person you decide to be"

Ralph Waldo Emerson

W I S E GOALS

MY MAIN GOAL RIGHT NOW

MY NO.1 GOAL IS... ....

TARGET DATE

How will I know I've reached my goal?
....
....

My key strengths that will help me achieve this goal are...
1. ....
2. ....
3. ....
4. ....
5. ....

This goal is important to me because...
♥ ♥ ♥ ♥ ♥ ♥
....
....
....
....

Obstacles that may arise are...
1. ....
2. ....
3. ....
4. ....
5. ....

How I plan to respond to each obstacle:
....
....
....
....
....

What will be different when I achieve my goal?
....
....
....
....

NEXT BEST STEPS
1. ....
2. ....
3. ....
4. ....
5. ....

© wisegoals.com

"The only person you are destined to
become is the person you decide to be"

Ralph Waldo Emerson

W I S E
GOALS

MY MAIN GOAL RIGHT NOW

MY NO.1
GOAL IS...

TARGET DATE

How will I know I've reached my goal?

My key strengths that will help me
achieve this goal are...
1.
2.
3.
4.
5.

This goal is important to me because...
♥ ♥ ♥ ♥ ♥ ♥

Obstacles that may arise are...
1.
2.
3.
4.
5.

How I plan to respond to each obstacle:

What will be different when I achieve
my goal?

NEXT BEST STEPS
1.
2.
3.
4.
5.

Printed in the United States
by Baker & Taylor Publisher Services